THE HARMONY

BETWEEN

CHRISTIAN FAITH

AND

PHYSICAL SCIENCE.

A Chapter of Christian Philosophy

BY

T. NELSON DALE, Jr.,

Author of "A Study of the Rhœtic Strata of the Val di Ledro in the Southern Tyrol."

PATERSON, N. J.:
"PRESS" BOOK AND JOB PRINT, 269 MAIN STREET.
1876.

RESPECTFULLY SUBMITTED

TO

THOSE PHILOSOPHICAL MINDS WHO ARE GRIEVED BY THE SOUND OF DISCORD

IN THE TEMPLE OF TRUTH.

"To conclude, therefore, let no man out of a weak conceit of sobriety, or an ill-applied moderation, think or maintain, that a man can search too far or be too well studied in the book of God's word, or in the book of God's works; divinity or philosophy; but rather let men endeavor an endless progress or proficience in both."

BACON: *Advancement of Learning.*

"His Son whom he hath appointed heir of all things by whom also he made the worlds."—HEB. 1, 2.

Some thoughtful minds, who hold enlightened views as to the *essential* harmony of religion and science, do not always discern the exact *method* of that harmony.

It will be readily granted that their profounder knowledge of both theological and physical science, and their better apprehension of the spirit and scope both of revealed religion and of science enable them to obtain a clearer view of their essential harmony. Their loyalty to common sense has also greatly aided them in obtaining such a view.

While comparatively little difficulty is experienced in recognizing the essential harmony of religion and science, the method of this harmony is not yet fully established in such questions as those of the Bible cosmogony and chronology, the creation of animal life and of man, the deluge, and the origin of languages.

These problems involve nearly all of the sciences, as well as the following theological questions: In what sense and to what extent the scriptures are inspired; how far they were designed to satisfy the craving of the human mind for knowledge; and also the question as to the exact principle which governs the treatment of second causes in the language of inspiration; and to what extent we ought to regard certain passages of the Old Testament as allegorical.

Such problems are so vast in their scope, and of such intellectual and religious consequence, that an exposition of any one of them which would satisfy both the theological and scientific intelligence, as well as the best christian sense of the day, would require more than a lifetime of profound, catholic and christian study. Indeed it may be said that the whole question of the relation of the natural to the supernatural in the cosmos of God, unsearchable as it is, is involved in these problems.

While these fields of study are so vast and beset with so many difficulties, there is a smaller field where not only the fundamental harmony between religion and science may be satisfactorily and briefly shown, but where also the method of that harmony may be viewed with the eye of a loving and intelligent faith.

It is that given in the title of this paper. While many of the questions between religion and science partake of a speculative character, this one is very practical in its bearings ; for the disastrous effect of an unbelieving science upon men render us suspicious of science ; and the fatal effect of a narrow-minded and ignorant faith upon science influences the mere scientist to turn a deaf ear to the appeal of evangelical christianity, and to seek to satisfy his spiritual nature with mere intellectual nourishment.

Avoiding scientific language, by *christian faith* is to be understood simply that filial attitude of the soul toward its Creator, which is made possible by the loving sacrifice and mediation of Jesus Christ, and is brought about in various ways by the gracious influence of the Divine Spirit.

We might stop here to consider at length the state of a man in such an attitude. It will be sufficient however to say that a man so disposed toward God is in a state of increasing harmony with himself physically, intellectually, and morally, as well as socially with his fellow-men, as far as in him lies, and above all with the benevolent character and will of his Maker. His complex being is brought under the gentle dominion of the precepts of Christ, and all his faculties gradually enter into their normal relations, and fulfill their appropriate offices. Coleridge describes the effect of christian faith as follows : " Never yet did there exist a full faith in the Divine Word, by whom light as well as immortality was brought into the world, which did not expand the intellect while it purified the heart; which did not multiply the aims and objects of the understanding, while it fixed and simplified those of the desires and passions."

While the christian enjoys the holy freedom implied in a filial relationship to his Divine Parent, the Giver of physical as well as moral law, and his mind and heart are expanded by his new hope, he looks upon nature with new interest. He verily recognizes God as its Maker, and sees in it the workmanship of God. He soon learns to praise God in His works. The evidences of Divine wisdom bring to his mind the evidences of Divine goodness. He may know little or nothing of the long train of intermediate causes by which God has fashioned the world and brought it to its present state of perfection and beauty, that is *how* God made it, but he knows that *somehow* God did make it, and that this God is his Father in Heaven.

Only when the christian beholds nature in the light of the cross does he fully realize and enjoy her beauty. The conscience relieved of its burden, the soul united forever to its Divine source and object, in harmony with itself looks upon nature with a sense of fellowship; for it recognizes that nature as well as its new life is of Divine origin, and the moral order and beauty within the soul respond to the physical order and beauty in nature.

With this spirit David's psalms abound. They were evidently written by one who not only communed with God, but was very familiar with His works. It is interesting to note how fully Alexander von Humboldt, Kosm. Vol. 2, p. 46, appreciated the truthfulness and grandeur of David's descriptions of nature. Would that he had told us as plainly that he loved their religious import also.

We have the words of our Lord himself contrasting the beauty with which God clothes a flower, with the pomp of human art, and it is safe to assert that it is a characteristic of the more intelligent and pious of God's children to be filled with devout admiration in the presence of His works.

Physical science may be briefly defined as that science which has primarily for its object the intellectual subjugation of nature in order that it may become the intellectual possession of man, independently of the possibility of that knowledge being made to contribute to his material welfare. More explicitly, its object is not only to obtain an encyclopædic knowledge of the physical world, but also a philosophical and historical knowledge of it, that is, an understanding of the laws which govern it, and of the relation of those laws to each other. Science endeavors to comprehend the system of second causes which operate in the physical world. Second causes may be defined as the ordinary means through which God acts in nature. The manner of their operation is then indirectly His manner. Physical science reveals the Divine method and manner in nature—that is the wisdom of God.

So that when the christian recognizes nature as the work of God, and not only devoutly admires it as such, but instinctively acknowledges that God fashioned it all in wisdom, physical science stands prepared to unfold to him that wisdom as far as she has ascertained it. He knows that God made and rules it *somehow* ; science tells him *how*. And thus when David says "O Lord how manifold are thy works! in wisdom hast thou made them all: the earth is full of thy riches," Ps. 104, 24, we may not perhaps be able to rise to the heights of worship to which David rose, but we may, with the aid of science, understand more of the import of his words than he could have understood.

There are a number of familiar passages in the scriptures in which the relation of Christ to the physical world is explained, and although it will not do to involve ourselves here in all the profound questions which centre about the Trinity, let us endeavor to form some simple, untheological conception of these passages as far as they have any interest to the ordinarily thoughtful christian mind.

The following passages will recur at once to the reader:

"The same was in the beginning with God, all things were made by him and without him was not anything made that was made."

"His Son whom he hath appointed heir of all things by whom also he made the worlds."

"And now O Father glorify thou me with thine own self with the glory which I had with thee before the world was."

From such passages we may infer that the same Being who took upon Him our sins, and carried our sorrows while in the flesh, had, while in the glory in which He had dwelt with the Father, made the physical universe.

Therefore as no soul enters Heaven without Him, so no blade of grass in the field, or shell upon the shore is without Him whom we call our Lord and Master. He is the visible link between the spiritual and physical Kingdoms of God. In Him centre all the mysteries both of godliness and of nature. The law of love and the law of nature proceed from Him. The revelations of science and the revelations of faith are revelations in the kingdoms of the one God and the one Word.

To illustrate this truth: Do we follow the scientist into all the minutiæ of his analysis, or back again as he builds up his magnificent synthesis, or do we accompany him as he patiently accumulates a vast number of concurrent facts, and then unfolds to us some great natural law, we are all the while but picking a cloth to pieces, thread by thread, or putting the same together again, thread by thread, or else reading the pattern according to which it was woven by a Divine workman.

Do we turn from this to the study of the beautiful character of some saintly christian matured by Divine grace for eternity, we are but examining another and a better work from the same Divine hand.

Or lastly, do we go to the inspired word, we there behold in the face of Jesus Christ the moral and personal character of the Divine workman himself, "full of grace and truth."

In the light of this doctrine, nature and the study of nature wear a more satisfactory aspect. For instance; in looking upon a mountain landscape, everybody is first impressed with its beauty, and the more the eye of the beholder has been trained to discern the beautiful, the greater will be his appreciation of the beauty of the scene. But if the beholder has a knowledge of geology he will, besides perceiving the beauty of form, color and perspective, understand the origin, history and structure of the mountains, and will thus comprehend the scientific significance of the scene.

He will not only understand and admire in themselves, the laws and operations of laws by which the mountains were formed, but he will consider the mountains also in their relation to the climate, irrigation and vegetation of the earth.

If in addition to an eye trained to discern beauty and a mind furnished with scientific knowledge, the person possesses a christian mind, he will see the wisdom of his Heavenly Father displayed in the origin, history, structure, effect and beauty of the mountains, and as he reflects upon it he will find that his æsthetical, philosophical, and religious natures are all harmonized and satisfied. This aspect would thus include all that a Ruskin, a Newton, a Humboldt, an Agassiz, or a Darwin have revealed to us of nature, complemented and sanctified by that which a David and a John beheld in it.

It will be readily seen what the practical effect of such an understanding of truth would be both upon christian faith and upon scientific pursuits.

Christian faith may well be *supplemented* by a knowledge of the wisdom of her God, and thus add the grace of intellectual humility to her graces of the heart, and afford herself even more grounds for intelligent worship and praise. And on the other hand, just as a knowledge of botany is incomplete without knowing the source of the heat and light which sustain vegetable life, so a knowledge of physical law needs to be *complemented* by a knowledge of the Giver of physical law, though reasons much more momentous and tender than this are not lacking to induce the scientist to seek Him whose physical law he so well understands.

The intellectual and religious satisfaction which the christian mind experiences, in view of the Divine wisdom as shown in the physical world, and the Divine goodness as shown in redeeming love, under the light of this truth could hardly be expressed in more fitting language than the following. (Language largely borrowed from another, originally used however to convey a cognate truth.)

"The reason, as well as the heart craves its sublime consolations.——Our thoughts find no rest until they soar upward and rest in God.——When I can say to myself with unfaltering lips, the physical world with all its laws and systems of laws, its past and future history, and every particle of organic and inorganic matter which it contains, and all forms of vegetable and animal life of the past and present, from the lowest to the highest are all the work of Divine wisdom, and that nothing of all these is untouched by the guiding and friendly hand of a merciful God and Redeemer—when I can say this what need is there of further argument? My heart is satisfied, for I have reached the issue of perfect benevolence; my reason is satisfied for I have reached the issue of perfect wisdom."

Nor has the world lacked instances where great beauty of christian character has been united to a life of devotion to, and eminent attainment in, physical science; although some of these christian scientists may not have clearly discerned the bond of union between their faith and their science, and others have felt it their duty to forsake the attractive field of scientific research to minister to the transcendent spiritual interests of their fellow men.

When we consider the self-denying and patient researches, the unswerving loyalty to truth, the love of exactitude, and that beautiful intellectual humility begotten of much knowledge, which are so characteristic of the true man of science, one might think it was but a step from these to the exalted christian morality set forth in the sermon on the mount and in the 13th Corinthians. But we must not forget that christian faith is the only solid foundation of christian morality.

We may gather some lessons of practical wisdom from the truth set forth. What should be the attitude of the christian toward physical science, especially at the present time? Certainly not one of enmity! Nor that of indifference either.

We may deeply regret that such and such a man whom God has endowed with capacity and opportunity to understand His works, may not feel his need of an intelligent christian faith; or that another may not guard language directed against a short-sighted interpretation of scripture from being understood as directed against inspiration itself; but we cannot refrain if we would from gladly welcoming the contributions of such men to scientific knowledge, or from admiring their intellectual gifts and acquirements.

The revelations of science are to the praise of God's wisdom. Let us therefore see to it that we be not found guilty of bringing a reproach upon God's benevolence by being too slow in recognizing His wisdom.

If science should by legitimate reasoning transfer the greater portion of the history of the physical universe from the domain of the supernatural into that of the natural, it will be no less Divine in its origin and development. Nor do the scriptures teach otherwise. What warrant have we for interpreting the simple figure of a workman, by which the Creator is generally represented to us in the Bible, as standing for one who did not make natural laws as tools to execute His concepts in that early morning of the world!

If christian thought should find herself compelled to admit a longer and wider reign of physical law than she has been wont, that law will lead her not less surely, because to her earthly vision less directly, to the Creator.

But even if we are unable to convince science of her need of God, we may insist that she shall be true to herself. As we insist upon morality in christian life, let us also insist upon a sound physical science and then cordially accept her revelations.

It is interesting to notice in this connection the protest which some of Professor Hæckels questionable data, hasty inferences, and unscientific language have called forth from scientists in Germany who speak in behalf of a pure science.

If physical science be but true to herself, she cannot fail of being true to God and to an enlightened interpretation of His word, and so unite with christian faith in the praise of Him who is the author of both.

We may then formulate the fundamental truth which should guide both christian and scientist in these words: *Jesus Christ the author and object of whatever degree of faith the christian may possess, is also the author of whatever physical law science may discover.* This foundation will stand the test of time and of eternity. And as between works of the same Divine mind there can be no discord, the spiritual and physical kingdoms of God are in perfect and beautiful harmony. But let the christian see to it that he understands the law of love as it is, and the scientist that he interprets the law of nature as it is.

If the great truth which has been set forth be borne in mind, and christian faith and physical science are true to their exalted missions as revealers of the *Divine Benevolence* and the *Divine Wisdom*, discord will cease to profane the temple of truth.

PATERSON, New Jersey, November 7th, 1876.

www.ingramcontent.com/pod-product-compliance
Lightning Source LLC
LaVergne TN
LVHW010833120826
845149LV00016B/1364
9781418190507